Whispers In The Wind

By
Echo Quinn

All Rights Reserved

Published By

Poets' Choice

www.poetschoice.in

Cover Designed By - Koni Deraz, Germany
Book Designed By - Mostafa Gad , Egypt
Edited By - Nicholas Lawrence Carter, USA

ISBN: 978-1-946211-66-8

BCID: 530-16361229

Price: $22.5 USD

First Edition

Love, Loss, and Heartbreak

For Poppy and Nanny

The Yellow Rose

Tears painted the page of my journal
Once again, as I picked up the pen
To write about my broken heart
Because I miss you
And we are far apart.

Earth and heaven separate us
I look up at the clouds every
day
And wonder what it must be
like
To be so far away.

The yellow roses on your grave
Had begun to wilt
When I finally had the courage
to come back;

Those flowers
They had been beautiful,
Just like your soul
But now, they were withered,
Faded and old.

I said a short prayer
Then turned to leave the grave,
When something crunched under my shoe;

I lifted my foot
And what I saw lying there
Made me realize
That your death
Wasn't more than I could bear;

I picked it up
The lone yellow rose
Admiring its fragile, blooming beauty

As held it in my hand
I began to understand
That it was going to be okay;

And just like those roses on your grave
My happiness should never fade away
But that I should be like that lone rose
Beautiful, strong, and brave.

You

You are my strength
Forever my song
You're the fire that lights within me;
You are my peace,
My home, and my comfort
My shelter from the storm.

Broken

Alone, I sit in the silence again
Sewing together
The pieces of my broken heart.
And no matter how many times
 I stitch it back together
It still feels broken in two.

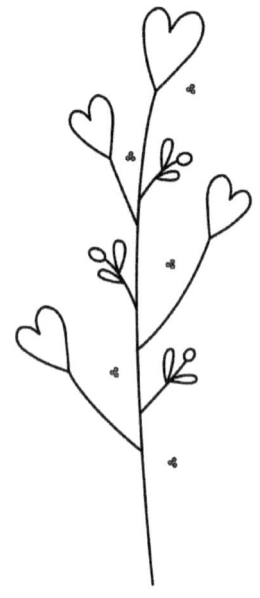

The Call

The stars never shone that night.
I sat, wide awake
In the worn leather chair,
Waiting for the call
That would break me.

Time passed excruciatingly slow;
It was nearly driving me insane
And I suppressed the urge to scream.
Hour after hour
I sat in the still silence
Waiting for that call-
The call that would break me.

Then, suddenly, I heard it, at last
Breaking through the silent, starless night
It sounded like shattered glass.

My chest felt tight,
I could hardly breathe
And a tear slipped down my cheek.
As I realized that the sound of the fragile, broken glass
Was my heart breaking in two.

Flawed

A knife through the heart
The thorns
Of betrayal
Twisting inside
The pain is tearing me apart
And I have no place to hide.

Discarded and flawed
I slowly turn away
Hoping that somehow
I'll find true love someday.

The Wind

The wind blew-
And everything changed;
It wasn't what I wanted
But the wind blew-
And everything changed.

The fields became empty and lifeless;
The sky, a stormy, dismal gray
The sun withdrew its warmth
And disappeared behind the clouds
When the wind blew that day.

The flowers, once beautiful and blooming
Wilted and faded away
My heart broke into a thousand pieces
When the wind blew that day.

The Door

Is anyone there
I am knocking at the door
Please let me in
I am weak; I am torn,
Feeling that I cannot stand
I need someone to take my hand
To hold me close
And whisper to me
Daughter, you will soon be free
Free to live and free to soar
You won't be tired or sick anymore
Your pain will be gone
You won't shed a tear
That is what I'm longing to hear;
Will you please let me in
I am knocking at the door
Weak and tired
I am wishing to soar.

Fire and Tears

You broke my heart
Like shattered glass
Scattered on the floor;
I fought back angry tears
As you walked out my door;
You never gave me a reason why
I felt that our love was a lie;

So I tore out that chapter
And burned it with the rest;
All the love letters, lies
And everything about us
I wanted to forget.

Fire and Scars

She wore her scars as a crown
A reminder of all she went through
And her battles yet to come;
But her wings were not broken
And even as the storm grew near
Still, she felt no fear;
Great determination swept over her soul
And with renewed strength, she picked up her sword and stepped into the fire once again.

Glass

I thought I was over it
That I'd found peace at last
But it came back and cut me
Like a sharp piece of glass.

The joy I once felt
Has now disappeared
Replaced with the deep pain
I had fought all those years.

I am sinking deep
No hope within
Fearing that I'll never know peace again;

I feel that this pain
Will never go away
It has wrapped itself around my heart
And I think it's here to stay.

Hope

Hope is within sight

For one day, I know

I'll be set free

Free from the bondage,

Free from the chains

And the darkness

Will no longer have a hold on me.

I'll be free to soar, free to fly

Free to live-

Instead of just existing.

Take My Hand

Take my hand
And go with me
To all the places
We have yet to see;
Be my anchor
As we weather the storm
My comfort, my shield
Hold me close keep me warm;
Be my fortress,
Light a fire in my soul
Together, my love, may we grow old.

Golden

The rising sun
Spills its golden rays
Through my bedroom window
And I wonder
What it must be like
To light up the world.

Soar

Rising from the ashes
She has conquered her fears
Her doubts and her pain
That she fought through the years
She's strong and hopeful
Her chains are now broken
She's free to soar.

Life

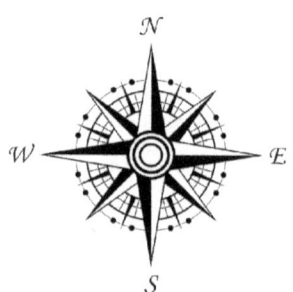

Let laughter and sunshine
Be your song
May love and light
Be your guide
As you live in the wondrous mystery
Of this journey called life.

A Perfect Storm

A perfect storm,
She was a delicate mixture
Of chaos and beauty
Her soul, a million diamonds
Her heart, a tangle of thorns.

Hidden

Hidden in a sea of self-doubt
Her soul, silently screaming for help
Waves of darkness clouded her mind
As inky shadows closed in from behind.

Shadows

Shimmering shadows
Haunt my dreams
As I lie, lost in a sea of spiderwebs
My soul aching
For just one peaceful night.

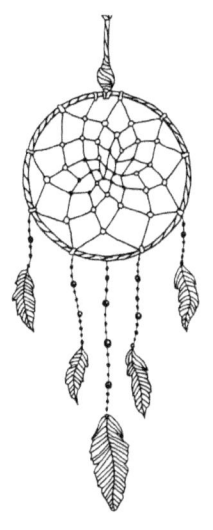

Drowned

Brutal words crushed her soul

Shattered into a thousand pieces

Waves of hurt

Drowned her heart

As she slowly slipped into the abyss of pair

Through Fire

I am not afraid to walk through the fire;
For I have you to show me the way.

Perfectly Imperfect

She carried her flaws
With beauty and grace;
Scars blanketed her soul
And pain twisted in her heart,
But she disregarded the judgmental stares
And persevered,
Because she was strong,
And no one knew
The battles she had fought,
No one knew the storms she had to walk through;
She knew she wasn't perfect,
And she would never be
But she believed in herself
And just like the rising sun,
She pressed on
Despite her flaws.

Mended Wings

Broken heart,

Ocean eyes

She soared on mended wings.

Smile

The savage storm rages

But yet I smile

And kiss my insecurities goodbye

Knowing that now

I'm free to fly.

Dancing in the Rain

You took my hand
And promised you'd be there
Forever and ever;

At my lowest
You wrapped me in your arms
And said
It's going to be okay;

Twirling in the good times
As well as the bad,
Forever-
Dancing in the rain with you.

Whispers in the Wind

Crimson leaves fall,
Scattering on the ground;
The wind whispers,
A comforting sound.

Peace

My love for you will never cease;
In you, I have found my peace.

The Mountain

Climbing the mountain,
Trying to reach the top
Though shadows pull me back
I will never stop.

Together

Stepping into the unknown
You hold my hand
We'll do this together
Though we don't understand.

Stars

The light of your love
Lifts me out of the shadows
Catapults me into the stars,
And gives me a ray of happiness
Beyond what I could have ever comprehended.

Darkness Into Light

There will be a day
When the shadows of this world
Will be banished
Feelings of fear, pain, and sorrow will disappear
And hopelessness will be a thing of the past.
The Light will defeat the Darkness
And open up a door of peace and love;
No longer will we tremble
No longer will we cower,
We will be strong,
We will have hope;
This dark world will be no more.

Light

Be the light in the darkness
So others may see
How bright you shine
How beautiful you can be.

Your Love

When you take my hand
The world stands still;
And the love you have for me
Is all that I feel.

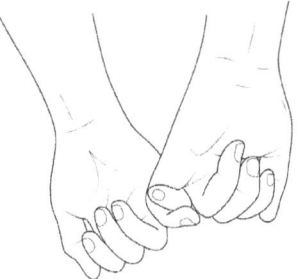

Snow

Snow crystals

Fall outside

As I sit by the window

In the silence

Watching the world go by.

Faith

Have faith

In what we cannot see

The answer will come;

Just wait and see.

Author's Note:

Thank you for picking up a copy of Whispers on the Wind. I hope you enjoyed reading it as much as I did writing it. Most of what I write comes from experiences in my life, and I've been writing since I was nine years old.

If you enjoyed this book, I have another anthology coming up soon titled "Beauty for Ashes: Poetry of Praise. I hope to have it available online by early spring of 2022.

Want to check out my writing progress? You can follow me on Instagram @echo_scribbles #echoquinnpoetry and I am also on Pinterest, Tumblr and Goodreads.

Happy reading!

    Love and light,

        Echo Quinn

Acknowledgements

I'd like to thank my family and friends for supporting me in my writing journey, especially

my husband, I wouldn't be where I am today without him.

Also, a special thank you to Poets Choice, for their help in the publishing process, and for all of their support and hard work putting the book together.

Our Authors

A Futile Attempt At Delaying The Inevitable By Adam Webb

Mr Daydream By Diana Willand

Preme Oka Kavithmaithe By Mohan Krishna Landa

Funnel To Freedoms Ring By Andre Brewer

Its Not About You By Jeremiah Valentine

Soft Reflection By Jamie Lim

Hashra By Abinash Singh Chib

Where Have All The Bluejays Gone by Jennifer Ayala

Sunlight Reflector By Sarah Cross

Whispers In The Wind By Echo Quinn

Questions We Didn't Ask Out Loud By Mars Hetherson

For Feedbacks:

Email – poetschoice@hotmail.com

Instagram - @poetschoice

Facebook – Poets Choice

Website – www.poetschoice.in / www.poetschoices.com

LinkedIn – Akshy Sonthalia

Twitter - @ppoetschoice

Youtube – Poets Choice

Also Published With Us In

www.ingramcontent.com/pod-product-compliance
Lightning Source LLC
Chambersburg PA
CBHW051134160426
43195CB00014B/2469